C'est La Vie, Mon Ami, C'est la Vie

C'est La Vie, Mon Ami, C'est la Vie

BETH HORVATH

Published in Australia by Sid Harta Books & Print Pty Ltd,
ABN: 34632585293
23 Stirling Crescent, Glen Waverley, Victoria 3150 Australia
Telephone: +61 3 9560 9920
E-mail: author@sidharta.com.au

First published in Australia 2021
This edition published 2021
Copyright © Beth Horvath 2021
Cover design, typesetting: WorkingType (www.workingtype.com.au)

The right of Beth Horvath to be identified as the
Author of the Work has been asserted in accordance with the
Copyright, Designs and Patents Act 1988.

All rights reserved. No part of this publication may be reproduced, stored in a retrieval system, or transmitted, in any form or by any means without the prior written permission of the publisher, nor be otherwise circulated in any form of binding or cover other than that in which it is published and without a similar condition being imposed on the subsequent purchaser.

Horvath, Beth
C'est La Vie, Mon Ami, C'est la Vie
ISBN: 978-1-925707-65-6
pp176

About the Author

Beth Horvath has been a musician for most of her 73 years. In her younger years, she was an actress in amateur dramatics.

She now lives a quiet life in a small river town with her lovely Hungarian husband.

Index of Poems

The Last Shot	1
Growing Old (Disgracefully)	4
The Talent Show	8
The Dreaded Flu	12
Wedding Day Blues	15
Four Short Poems	18
Freedom	20
Sea Change	22
The Old Girl	24
No Regrets — One Man's Odyssey	28
My Boy	33
Last Tango in Goolwa	37
Birds-1	41
Birds-2	43
Arcadia	46
The Karaoke King	63
Champagne Charlie	66

Champagne Charlie – The Sequel	71
Our House	76
Our House – 2	80
The Busker	83
A Place in The Sun	87
Mrs Brown	93
Ship Ahoy Mrs Brown	97
Mamma Mia Mrs Brown	105
Bon Voyage Mrs Brown	112
Dapper Dan	118
The Greedy Widow	123
Franklin Fife's Folly	126
The Soldier's Wife	130
Why?	137
Maybe	140
Reminiscence	145
The Quirky Tale of Quentin Quail	151
Our Love	155
The Old Man	157
She	159
Friendship	161
Memories	163
Two Different Worlds	166
Through My Window	168

The Last Shot

They're playing indoor bowls today
at the Dublin Social Club;
The whiskey's flowing freely,
there's lots of lovely grub.

The game is almost over,
two shots left to play;
Some bowlers are quite knackered,
it's been a tiring day.

Murphy steps up, takes his place,
wipes the sweat from his weathered face;
His days of glory are long past,
but he'll try his best to the very last.

His bowl's delivered down the mat;
'Oh no,' he groans, 'dear Lord not that.'
It's the worst shot ever seen,
very fast and too much green.
'Never mind,' his team-mates say,
'you've had some gutsy shots today.'

Last to bowl is Big Maureen,
who thinks she is the bowling queen;
Her Irish eyes aren't smiling
and she's looking very mean.

Casey bellows, 'Come this way!'
She glares at him, 'No not today.
You've done your bit, I'll do the rest,
for after all, I'm still the best.'
Casey mutters, 'Bloomin' pest.'

Her shot must count, it can't be crook,
poor old Murphy cannot look;
She takes her time, her aim is true,
'I'll show you mugs what I can do.'

The bowl runs straight but it's the shot,

    she's taken out Spud Murphy's lot;

She's persevered, 'Well done, hear, hear.'

    Now for a whisky and a chaser of beer.

For sure and begorra it's been a good day

    at the Dublin Social Club;

Where the whisky flows like water,

    and they serve the best Irish grub.

Growing Old (Disgracefully)

My kids tell me I'm getting old,
and a bit forgetful too;
I haven't any grey hairs yet,
well maybe just a few.

I still wear jeans and miniskirts,
and love to rock 'n roll;
But gee it's been an eternity,
since a fella's called me 'Doll.'

I don't have any wrinkles,
but I guess one day I will,
So I'll have to grab the bull by the horns
and take a little pill.

It's advertised on tele,
a wonder drug they say;
But I'll need quite a few,
I'm telling you, to keep those lines at bay.

I really don't feel older;
well not much anyway,
I haven't lost my marbles,
and my bones are still okay;
They haven't creaked for at least a week,
or was that yesterday?

I'd love to go on Tinder
and snag a red hot beau;
But when I asked my kids for help
they didn't want to know.

My children are so mean to me,
but they'll be sorry, yes siree;
I'll get revenge, it won't take long,
soon they'll be singing a different song.

I've joined the local nudist club
and dyed my hair bright green;
The old blokes there adore me,
they treat me like a queen.

I'm a cool recycled teenager,
I tell my kids for fun,
and I smile to myself as they moan and groan,
'Mum's been too long in the sun.'

Yesterday I took the plunge,
I got myself a tat:
The kids were shocked,
'Mum must be mad to pull a stunt like that.'

They carried on like lunatics,
it was just a little rose;
So I shocked them even further,
and got an earring in my nose.

I'm growing old disgracefully
and having lots of fun;
My family can't keep up with me,
I've got them on the run.

But I've heard they've checked out
nursing homes,
I'll have to keep my wits,
so I've promised to behave myself
and join the Senior Cit's.

Though the oldies might not want me there,
when I rock up with bright green hair,
groovy tattoos everywhere,
and an earring in my nose.

But they won't see me for ages,
I'll make a bucket list instead,
and do all the things that I've not done before,
because as I've always said,
'You've got to live life to the fullest,
for you're a long time dead.'

The Talent Show

I'm going on a talent show,
my favourite one at that;
I've bought a sparkly dress to wear,
I hope I won't look fat.

I've got a brand new hairdo,
dreadlocks dyed fluorescent blue
to cover up the grey;
For sure I'll be an instant hit,
when I rock up today.

My old man thinks I'm bonkers,
the family all agree;
They hate my hair but I don't care,
I'm happy as can be;
Soon I'll be on tele,
for all the world to see.

It really was quite daunting
on that talent show;
The judges didn't fancy me,
they told me where to go.

Three of them were not too bad,
the fourth one was quite rude;
He didn't like my singing,
and thought my jokes were crude.

I got four buzzers, dear oh dear,
but I'll be back again next year;
I'll not be beaten just you see,
Mr Cowell you don't scare me.

My children were embarrassed,
to see me on TV.
But I was not at all upset,
it didn't bother me.

I've found myself an agent,
and I have a fancy name;
I hope to crack the big time,
and find forever fame.

I'm known as Nitro Nanny,
man, I love that name.
Doing gigs in Nursing Homes,
I'm a busy little dame.

The oldies love my naughty jokes,
and heavy metal songs.
They're bored to death with bingo games,
and tired of sing-alongs.

I've since been banned from Nursing Homes,
'Too risqué,' they said.
So now I'm entertaining folk,
in pubs and clubs instead.

My useless hubby's done a bunk,
but why should this chick care?
I'm raking in the money,
soon I'll be a millionaire.

My audiences love me,

they scream and yell for more;

So eat your heart out Simon Cowell,

you really are a bore.

You may have won the battle,

but this old girl's won the war.

I'll never need to bother,

with your talent quest.

You brought me down but I survived,

and brother I'm the best.

The Dreaded Flu

The dreaded flu has struck again,
even though I tried in vain
to keep the enemy from the door,
it marched right in and declared 'It's war!'
Oh me, oh my what can I do,
to chase away this dreaded flu?

My schnozzle runs, my poor eyes weep,
I toss and turn; Why can't I sleep?
The doc says, 'Not much I can do,
to help you beat this wretched flu.
Go home, have a whisky and a Panadol or two.
But don't forget to pay my bill,
in case you don't pull through.'

I feel as if my head will burst,
this cough must surely be the worst
that anyone has ever had,
I want to die I feel so bad.
My family have no sympathy
for poor sick and sorry me.

I've countless potions, pills as well,
to kill this ghastly bug from hell;
But it just will not go away,
it torments me both night and day.

It's stuck to me like super glue,
I can't shake off this horrid flu;
I'm sure I'll soon be at death's door,
I cannot take it anymore!
Please God help me win this war.

I'm cold, I'm hot, oh I don't know,
I'm so depressed and very low,
I've gone and lost my appetite;
I'm such a mess, an awful sight.
Oh dreaded flu won't you take flight,
so I can make it through the night.

Morning's here and with the sun,
I've got the enemy on the run.
That worthless good-for-nothing flu
has hit the road, said Toodle-oo;
I'm not sad to see it go,
my uninvited heartless foe.

Don't you dare come back next year,
you won't be very welcome here.
Goodbye, Adieu oh dreaded flu.
You might miss me but I won't miss you,
I've won the war and we're finally through.

Wedding Day Blues

Our Aggie's getting married,
she's happy as a lark;
She met a bonza bloke last week,
while walking in the park.

Our Aggie's getting married,
her ship's come in at last;
The poor girl's never had much luck
with fellas in the past.

She was once engaged to a terrible flirt,
he'd chase after anything in a skirt;
Treated little Ag. like dirt,
but she was blinded by love.

He proposed and she said yes,
we weren't amused I must confess;
The wedding day dawned clear and bright,
we drove her to the church;
Hoping she would see the light
and leave him in the lurch.

But Aggie wouldn't listen,
and angry words were said;
She told us explicitly where to go,
and the nuptials went ahead.

As Aggie drifted up the aisle,
we couldn't even crack a smile.
But oh she looked a picture,
the bridegroom deathly white;
It must have been some stag do,
at the 'Rose And Crown' last night.

The preacher cried, 'Do you take this bride,
with love and pride, to be your wife,
your trouble and strife?'
The groom got cold feet, he took to the street,
screaming, 'No, not on your life!'

Our little girl was very sad,
but she should have heeded Mum and Dad;
We told her that the bloke was bad;
a fly-by-night, a worthless cad.

'String 'im up!' the people cried,
while the preacher shook his head
and sighed,
'That little girl was never meant
to be a blushing bride.'

But he was wrong, we're glad to say,
our Aggie tied the knot today;
She's off our hands at last.
No more tantrums, no more noise,
no more late night calls from boys.

Our baby girl has flown the nest,
left the warmth of her mother's breast;
But at sixty she should know what's best.
Thank God she's finally married!

Four Short Poems

There once was a bowler called Nat,
who fancied a sheila named Kat.
When she waddled by,
he would utter a sigh
and send all his bowls off the mat.

There was a young bowler called Jean,
her skirts were so short 'twas obscene.
The ladies said, 'Ban her.'
The fellas cried, 'No.'
The ayes won the toss and young Jean had to go.

There was an old bowler called Mabel,
the poor thing was clearly unstable.
When her team didn't win,
she'd scream, 'That's a sin!'
How very unsporting of Mabel.

There was a young fellow from Fife,
who loved another man's wife.
They got caught in bed,
now they're both stone cold dead,
and hubby is banged up for life.

Freedom

I'm on top of the world, my troubles are few,
as I follow the road with my faithful dog, Blue;
We go where life takes us, unfettered and free,
best mates forever, old Bluey and me.

Oh give us a home where the Wallaby roam,
where the Wombat and Echidna play;
Where often is heard, the shrill cry of a bird,
as it flies through the tree tops all day.

I tramp with my swag on my back,
along a winding bush track;
Old Bluey and me, how we love to be free,
in the bush or the dusty outback.

Yes give us a home where the Wallaby roam,
where the Emu and Kangaroo play;
Where often is heard, the shrill cry of a bird,
as it flies through the tree tops all day.

We'll wander this land till we die,
for it's here our hearts truly lie;
My best mate and me, we'll forever be free,
under a southern blue sky.

So give us a home where the Wallaby roam,
Where the Bilby and Bandicoot play;
Where often is heard, the shrill cry of a bird,
as it flies through the tree tops all day.

Sea Change

There's a tiny white-washed cottage,
in a quiet seaside town;
Where a bonza lass, the lovely Maude,
has finally settled down.

She used to be a gypsy,
roaming our great land;
Until a hero came along
and took her by the hand.

He crooned sweet nothings in her ear,
'Won't you stay with me?'
So she followed her heart
and went with him to his cottage by the sea.

He's become her soulmate,
a handsome caring bloke;
He treats her like a princess,
and loves to tell a joke.

He's her knight in shining armour,
    a tender loving man;
He pens her love poems every day,
    and Maude's his biggest fan.

He serenades her every night,
    that dude is really good;
He ought to be in show biz,
    at least Maude thinks he should.

She never wants for anything,
    he's such a generous guy;
They live life to the fullest,
    as the sands of time drift by.

Maude has found her place in the sun,
    she loves the seaside life;
Far removed from the world she knew,
    as a vagabond gypsy's wife.

I hope they'll be together,
    forever fancy-free;
In that tiny white-washed cottage,
    where the river meets the sea.

The Old Girl

I came across her in the crowded bar
of a pub in a small country town;
Through the smoky haze she beckoned to me,
'Come sit here Buddy, this stool is free,
buy me a beer and we'll talk for a while.'
So I sat myself down and she gave me a smile.

She was wrinkled and grey with a firm steely gaze,
in an old woollen coat that had seen better days;
I bought her a beer and she said with a tear,
'I'm not much to look at, I'm old and so tired,
my use-by-date has long expired;
But in a past life I was loved and admired.'

She showed me a photo from a long time ago,
a beautiful girl and her handsome young beau;
Then another; a groom and his radiant bride;
'So many memories,' she wistfully sighed.

She spoke of the good times along with the bad,
of laughter and mateship, but then she grew sad;
She sobbed as she told me of bushfires
and drought,
and how her young farmer could see no way out.

His dreams for their future were ebbing away,
the black dog was biting day after day;
Life was a burden, sorrow and strife,
so one winter's morn he farewelled his wife,
Rode into the forest and ended his life.

Now he sleeps forever in a quiet place,
as time drifts slowly by;
Where wildflowers greet the morning sun,
and ghost gums hug the sky.

One bleak sombre day his heartbroken wife
knelt by his graveside to pray;
'Dear Lord when you see my beloved,
will you tell why I couldn't stay?'

'Please explain to him Lord,
how I fought the good fight,
but I had to call it a day;
When faceless men with hearts of stone,
stole his birthright away.'

We drank through the night
and I felt her pain,
as she told her sad story all over again;
I left her to ponder why life is unfair,
why sorrow and heartache
are so hard to bear.

Sometimes at night when the moon's
on the rise,
I dream of a girl with emerald
green eyes;
and the handsome young farmer
with whom her heart lies.

One day I returned to that crowded bar,
but the old girl had gone away;
With a joyful heart she left this world,
one glorious autumn day.

Now she sleeps with her beloved,

where ghost gums hug the sky;

and wildflowers bloom in profusion,

As time drifts slowly by.

No Regrets
One Man's Odyssey

When I was a young man,
I led a shallow life;
I had a high-powered job, a penthouse
and a pampered selfish wife.

One day I left it all behind,
abandoned my sad worthless life;
Packed my bags and hit the road,
said goodbye to my beautiful wife.

I now live my life as a nomad,
a gypsy, a swaggie; true blue;
The road is my home;
I'm free, so I roam.

I owe the world nought,
I'm a fortunate man;
I go where I please,
whenever I can.

I've played my guitar
to a half-empty bar,
in a rundown outback pub;
For the princely sum of a stubby or two,
and a plate of the finest grub.

I've been a smithy and a handyman,
a roadie for a band;
Hitched many a ride with truckies,
to cross this wide brown land.

I've been a jackaroo, a drover,
toiled in a shearing shed;
But underneath a southern sky,
is where I make my bed.

One night in the eerie silence,
by the timeless deep blue sea,
a dark-haired ebon woman gently came to me;
She told me of her people, their dreamtime,
and their lands;
I closed my eyes and listened,
as we lay upon the sands.

Then like a shadow she slipped away,
into the hallowed night,
and I slept the sleep of a peaceful man,
till the early morning light;
And now as I traverse this sunburnt land,
I feel her spirit close at hand.

I've smelt the acrid stench of death
from bushfires out of hell;
I've witnessed mighty cyclones,
flooding rains as well.

I've seen the pain in a farmer's eyes
and felt his suffering too,
as he weeps at the thought of walking away,
to start his life anew.

The drought has taken everything
his ancestors held dear;
But he's a born survivor,
he'll be back so never fear.

I've stood beneath the Southern Cross,
on a dry and treeless plain;
Fell to my knees and prayed to God,
to send some precious rain;
If my prayers would just be answered,
the grass might grow again.

When my days on earth are over,
and I'm finally laid to my rest,
take me back to Paradise,
to the place I loved the best.

Where the deep blue ocean waters
meet the shifting silver sands,
where a brown-eyed native woman
gently held my hands.

Where wild dolphins play
in the heat of the day
and sea birds take flight
in evening's cold light.

Scatter my ashes
from somewhere on high,
into the sunset,
through the night sky;
So I'll soar like an eagle,
majestic and free,
for this is the way that I want it to be;
No sad songs, no headstone, no eulogy.

I'll leave this big country
the way that I came,
I never had riches,
nor did I have fame;
A drifter, a dreamer,
a man with no name.

My Boy

Memories of days gone by,
come flooding back to me;
As I sit in contemplation,
beneath the old gum tree.

So many wondrous times we've had,
my faithful Jim and me;
Through blazing sun and gentle rain,
under that old gum tree.

When we weren't resting under our tree,
life was exciting for Jimmy and me;
We'd climb mountains and sand dunes,
bathe in the sea;
We'd dance in the rain, so happy and free,
we were never apart, my best mate and me.

We'd laze by the fire on a cold winter's night,
listen to music till dawn's early light;
Sleep in till noon, watch soaps on TV,
as happy as Larry,
my Jimmy and me.

One day I awoke to a grey dismal morn,
Jim lay beside me so still and forlorn;
Something was wrong, things looked very grim,
I felt scared and alone; afraid for my Jim.

The doctors said gently, 'We'll try our best,
to help him get well,
but he'll need lots of rest.'

'He's a brave little fighter,
we're sure he'll pull through.
Come back tomorrow, there's nought you can do.'

I slowly returned to my cold lonely room,
and sat there in the silence, the stillness and gloom;
I called to the angels, 'Please hear my prayer,
don't take my Jimmy, it wouldn't be fair.'

'He's not harmed a soul, he's never been bad,
Jim's just a boy, a wee Aussie lad.'
I finally slept for a few hours that night,
to suddenly wake in the cold morning light.

Then came the news I'd been waiting to hear,
'Your boy has pulled through,
there's no need to fear.
He rallied around to our utmost joy,
he sure is a battler, your tough Aussie boy.'

With his wagging tail and soft silky hair,
he's the love of my life, my Jimmy so fair;
His coat's a bit greyer, his eyes have gone dim,
but he's just like a puppy,
my little scamp Jim.

He's not very agile but neither am I,
so we sit in the sunshine and watch life go by;
He looks up at me with his melting brown eyes,
my faithful companion, so loving and wise.

Two golden oldies, Jimmy and me,
under the shade of our precious gum tree;
But time marches on, especially for Jim,
and one day I'll have to bid farewell to him;
Then I'll lay him to rest where he'll always be free,
under the shade of that mighty gum tree.

When my time has come and I've said my goodbyes,
please take my remains to where my heart lies;
Where a four-legged, loveable silky-haired boy
gave me his heart and brought me much joy;
Scatter my ashes so I'll always be
under the shade of the ancient gum tree.

In loving memory of Scrappy – 1998-2011.
'A little bloke with a big heart.'

Last Tango in Goolwa

A silver-haired Hungarian
was searching for romance,
and every week he'd try his luck
at a popular singles dance.

He was a hit with the ladies there,
so well-groomed and debonair;
From the cut of his smart Italian suit,
to the sheen of his silvery hair.

But he wasn't so keen on the ladies,
who frequented the dance;
He would much prefer a younger dame,
with a hankering for romance.

One night there came into the place,
a lass with auburn hair;
She spied the suave Hungarian,
and tried hard not to stare.

But their eyes connected across the room,
his heart beat faster, *Boom, Boom, Boom*;
He asked her would she like to dance,
and that was the start of a lasting romance.

The old girls at the singles club
were mournful as can be,
'cause the smooth Hungarian Romeo
was no longer free.

He's found himself a lady
to share his lonely life,
and very soon she would become
his ever-loving wife.

They married in the springtime,
almost two years to the day;
When he walked across that crowded room
and took her breath away.

Twenty years have come and gone,
and they're still together;
Living life to the fullest,
no matter what the weather.

They've travelled to exotic lands,
seen wealth and poverty;
Frolicked on the golden sands
by the Adriatic Sea.

They've marvelled at the sunrise,
from a snow-clad peak on high;
Gazed in awe at the shimmering moon,
in an ebon Paris sky.

They've sheltered in a small café
from the misty summer rain;
Danced to Gypsy violins,
falling in love once again;
Wandered the streets of Budapest,
in the early morning light;
All was well in their universe,
everything was alright.

But then it was time for a tree change,
a new chapter in their life,
for the silver-haired Hungarian
and his loyal Aussie wife.

They stayed a while in Tassie,

then a bustling South East town;

But they still were not contented,

they couldn't settle down.

So they followed the long and winding road

and found their destiny,

where the mighty Murray River

meets the deep blue sea.

Now it's farewell to our lovebirds,

and may they always be

filled with the joy of living,

in their haven by the sea.

Birds-1

The kiwi leads a boring life,
it comes out late at night;
The poor thing doesn't do much else,
it just stays out of sight.

We seagulls have a grand old time,
lazing on the sand;
Gobbling lots of scrummy food,
we're such a happy band.

Floating on the briny sea,
calling to our friends;
Screeching with excitement,
the fun just never ends.

We seagulls are a handsome lot,
the prettiest of birds;
When people see our beauty,
they're almost lost for words.

We're 'Aussie Eco Warriors,'
and we work hard each day;
Cleaning up the rubbish tip
down Victor Harbor way.

So eat your heart out, kiwi bird,
your mob can't even fly;
You'll be a party-pooper,
until the day you die.

Birds-2

The kiwi bird unlike the seagull
doesn't have much fun;
You won't find it catching waves
or basking in the sun.

It's too busy bringing up
it's little family,
far away from Aussie shores
across the Tasman Sea.

The people of the Shaky Isles
adore their kiwi bird;
So unique in every way,
seldom seen or heard.

But if you visit wildlife parks
or zoos across the land;
You might be very fortunate
to see some close at hand.

Back across the Tasman Sea,
in the land of green and gold;
Our national living treasures
are a wonder to behold.

Koala in the old gum tree,
(don't call it a bear);
The not-so-cuddly platypus,
a creature oh so rare.

The naughty little seagulls
are definitely not rare;
They're still creating havoc everywhere,
playing chasey on the sand
beneath the burning sun,
swiping greasy fish and chips
annoying everyone.

I'm sure that if I were a bird
a kiwi I would be,
living life in paradise
with my family.

But then perhaps a seagull's life
might be the way to go;
Flirting with the pretty girls,
putting on a show;
With lots of free meals to be had,
a seagull's life can't be so bad.

Little kiwi live your life in peace and harmony;
Far away from prying eyes in your sanctuary
and seagull please don't change your ways,
you're okay as you are,
even though you drive us mad,
we think you are a star.

Arcadia
A place of rustic contentment and simplicity.

I sit back on my old front porch,
in quiet reverie;
Gossamer clouds float gently by,
as the blazing sun greets the indigo sky.

The winds of time blow softly,
o'er the distant plain;
While somewhere in the vast outback,
a farmer prays for rain.

I am a man of simple means,
no worldly goods have I;
It's a meagre unspoiled life I lead,
under a southern sky.

My house is just a run-down shack,
but it's home sweet home to me;
A refuge from the world beyond,
a hallowed sanctuary.

I left the world I used to know,
the place I loved so well;
That once for me was a paradise,
but is now a living hell.

I once was a preacher, a man of God,
but my faith was shattered one day;
When my prayers to the Lord went unanswered,
and young lives were taken away;
Innocent men caught up in a war,
far removed from their native shore.

In my unrelenting nightmares,
my never-ending dreams,
I can still smell the rotting flesh
and hear the piercing screams
of comrades who were left to die;
Cut down in their prime,
forever young and innocent,
immortalised in time.

I still can hear their voices,
begging, crying out to me,
'In God's name put an end to this,
please father, set us free.'

But there was nothing I could do
to help them on their way,
except to hold them close to me,
dry their eyes and pray.

So I prayed to God to put an end
to this crazy, hopeless war,
'Won't you hear my humble plea,
as you always have before?'
But he couldn't have heard,
for the conflict raged on,
so many lives were forever gone.

I came back from the war,
a sad, empty shell,
like so many others, I'd been through hell.
But the country we'd all sworn allegiance to,
was not the same as before.
No welcoming arms; we were outcasts and lepers,
because of a cruel Asian war.

So I vowed I'd leave the world behind,
to find my place in the sun,
far away from the madding crowds,
'till my final race has been run.
I sit back in contentment,
and watch the world go by;
I marvel at the glorious arc
of a rainbow in the sky.

When the daylight hours have come and gone,
like the cooling summer rain;
When the evening shadows deepen,
it's then I feel the pain.

As the swirling mist comes rolling in,
across the treeless plain;
The horrors of the past return,
to haunt me once again.

I mourn the valiant dauntless souls,
the ones who went before;
Young lives lost so needlessly,
in a bloody Asian war.

In my nocturnal wanderings,
through the unforgiving night,
a myriad of silver stars
forever shining bright;
Guide weary-laden travellers
with an incandescent light.

I wonder if the vale of tears
that I left so long ago,
Is still the same as it was before,
but I guess I'll never know.

I'm contented in my Eden,
but I sometimes feel alone;
Once in a while my weary heart longs
for a soulmate of my own.

By chance a jaded pilgrim,
from a country far away,
Stopped to rest her weary bones,
on a foggy winter's day.

She was no classic beauty,
but oh those Irish eyes,
They sparkled like a million stars,
in the dark ethereal skies.

Her smile, so warm and tender,
would melt the coldest heart,
Her inner beauty shone right through
and I loved her from the start.

I listened to her throughout the day,
as she spoke of her deep despair.
The things that she told me,
such dark dreaded tales,
were more than I could bear.
I cried out in anger and wondered again
why life was unfair; so full of pain;
The world was in turmoil as never before;
Brave men still die in the theatres of war.

In a hell-hole where drought and famine reign,
children scream out in hunger and pain;
Women are raped, again and again;
Boy soldiers fight in an unholy war;
Slavery is rife, just as before,
and corrupt politicians couldn't care less
that their country is in such a terrible mess.

While the idle rich laze back in their chairs,
and dream of becoming millionaires;
They eat fancy food and guzzle champagne,
but with all that they have, they still complain
while the homeless freeze in the driving rain.

But sometimes good men came along
and tried to save the world;
Stout-hearted unsung warriors, brave and true,
who lifted sad forgotten souls
from depths of dark despair
when others turned their backs on them,
and no-one seemed to care.

In her heartache and her sorrow,
her never-ending pain,
She vowed that she would not set foot
in the outside world again.
But even through the tear-drops,
she still could find a smile,
'This place seems like a paradise,
May I stay here for a while?'

She shared my nights and morning days,
she changed my life in many ways.
The terrifying dreaded dreams
diminished through the years;
When I was sad she held me close
and wiped away the tears.

She made me happy once again,
she helped me fight my inner pain,
the heartaches and the fears,
and I thought that she was happy too,
throughout those timeless years.

Perhaps I'd been too selfish,
expecting her to stay,
for I found her crying needlessly
on a golden autumn day.

I knew that she would leave one day,
she never really meant to stay.
'Just a little while,' she said.
Her heart belonged to someone else,
far across the sea;
So I had to be stronger than ever before,
I had to set her free.

The days are growing shorter,
the nights are cold and long;
Soon autumn will be over,
and I'll hear old winter's song.

Sometimes I dream about her,
through the solitary night,
I feel her body close to mine,
in the shimmering morning light.

Perhaps she was an angel,
sent down from heaven above,
to fill my life with happiness,
and unconditional love.

I pray that she'll come back again,
and end this unrelenting pain
that plays upon my heartstrings
like a broken melody;
That haunts my every waking hour,
and never sets me free.

Someone must have heard my plea,
for one day she returned to me
from the Emerald Isles of her childhood,
beyond the Irish Sea,
where she'd cared for her dying mother,
until the day she was finally free.

The dear one who turned on her heart light;
Her mother who gave so much love,
now was at peace in the arms of the angels,
in a far better place up above.

But before the sands of time ran out,
before her final dreamless sleep,
she opened her weary eyes and smiled,
'My darling, please don't weep.
My pain will soon be over,
at last I shall be free.
Don't be sad, be happy,
each time you think of me.'

Her broken-hearted daughter
promised not to mourn,
as she held her tight throughout the night,
until the break of dawn.

In a tiny white-washed cottage,
somewhere near Galway Bay,
she watched her precious mother's life
slowly ebb away.

But she could not leave her buried there,
in a lonely grave with no-one to care;
That would have been too much to bear,
yet she knew deep down in her innermost soul,
if she were to tear her away
from Erin's green hills and valleys,
it would haunt her every day,
for her mother's heart will always lie,
under that infinite blue sky.

As she gazed upon the setting sun
in all its majesty
and the transient birds of passage,
untamed, eternally free,
she realised then what she had to do,
before coming home to me.

In a peaceful country churchyard,
where emerald shamrocks grow,
sheltered from the driving rain
and the alabaster snow,
she left a part of her loved one there
where her heart would always be,
in her beloved homeland,
on the shores of the Irish Sea.

The rising sun signalled a brand new day,
over the shores of Galway Bay;
'Rest in peace, my angel heart,
I promise not to cry.'
Then it was time to take her leave,
but not to say goodbye.

She carried her mother's precious remains
over the sapphire sea
to our little piece of paradise,
our blessed sanctuary,
where once in the past, a lifetime ago,
she had found solace with me.

We buried her mother's ashes,
where the golden wattles grow,
where wild flowers bloom in springtime,
and gentle breezes blow;
Across the misty mountains,
to the valley down below.

Where the laughing kookaburras
greet the morning sun,
and the skylark sings at heaven's gate,
when the day is done.

We smiled through our tears
as we said our goodbyes,
for her mother was finally free,
to rest in everlasting peace,
for all eternity.

We vowed as we left those hallowed grounds,
that we'd never again be apart;
It was time to fulfil all the dreams we once had,
a fresh beginning, a brand new start;
I would have to erase those indelible memories,
still etched upon my heart.

Father Time is marching on,
we're growing older now;
The ugly nightmares of the past
have disappeared somehow.

For when I thought all hope had gone,
she gave me strength to carry on;
She drove away the demons
that had plagued me for so long.

We count our blessings day by day,
so grateful we are still here,
living in peace and harmony,
free from doubt and fear;
Away from the mad frenetic pace
of a self-indulgent human race.

When our journey's end is near,
we will cross the great divide,
to that blessed world beyond the grave,
on our last magic carpet ride.

When the music of life has faded away,
and it's time for us to call it a day,
we'll leave behind a legacy,
a handsome, brown-eyed boy;
The apple of his father's eye,
his mother's pride and joy.

But we know he'll never be alone,
for he's found a sweetheart of his own;
A girl with music in her soul,
passed by our door one day,
and fearful of the world outside,
she asked if she might stay.

Just as another traveller,
from far across the sea
once stopped to ask,
'May I stay for a while?'
and fell in love with me.

As time goes by in Arcadia,
there's a new life in our clan;
An adorable bundle of happiness,
a precious little man.

They say God giveth and taketh away,
and thus it was on a bleak winter's day;
My beloved and I said our final farewells,
uttered one last goodbye,
before we left our dear ones
for that mansion in the sky.

But our earthly remains will be scattered
where gentle breezes blow,
across the majestic mountain
to the valley far below,
where the wild flowers bloom in profusion
and the golden wattles grow.

Where the laughing kookaburras,
salute the rising sun,
and the skylark serenades the moon,
when the day is done.

The Karaoke King

He's the King of Karaoke,
the Chairman of the Board;
When he croons their favourite tunes,
the crowds are overawed.

He's the King of Karaoke,
cool and fancy free;
When he walks by,
the ladies cry,
'Harry marry me.'

But Harry likes the single life,
he doesn't need a nagging wife.
He's here tonight to give his fans
a show they won't forget;
The other acts have come and gone,
he's still the greatest yet.

The lights are dimmed,
the crowd is hushed;
He takes his time,
he'll not be rushed.

Then the room erupts with a mighty cheer,
he's singing a song that they hold so dear;
The place is filled with emotion,
even tough men shed a tear.

Ol' Blue Eyes did it his way,
and Harry does it too;
He'll be around for a long, long time,
to sing his tunes for you.

One day we'll have to bid farewell
to the Karaoke King;
But we'll never forget those immortal songs
that he always used to sing.

I'm sure he will be somewhere
on that big stage in the sky;
Singing a duet or two with Frank,
as time goes slowly by.

Swingin' with the Rat Pack
on a distant star;
Good on you Karaoke King,
you were the best by far.

Champagne Charlie

In a brownstone house in Paris,
lives a charismatic man;
His name is Champagne Charlie,
Sinatra's greatest fan.

He has a pretty wife, Marie,
and they live in perfect harmony
in their brownstone in Paris,
near the Rue de Rivoli.

He used to be a singer
at a Paris cabaret;
But times are tough,
the crowds have gone,
the music has faded away;
The final curtain has fallen;
It was time to call it a day.

Now Champagne Charlie's on the dole,
there's nothing much to do;
So he keeps the neighbours entertained,
with a classic song or two.

The neighbours are quite happy,
they love a Sinatra tune;
He serenades them every day
with 'Fly Me to The Moon.'

'My Way,' is their favourite,
he can sing that all day long;
But his little wife is sick and tired
of hearing that endless song.

'Why don't you move your derriere,
go somewhere else to sing?
Try a little busking,
I've heard it's just the thing.'

'You need to earn some money,
there's not much coming in;
I really need some peace and quiet
from your awful din.'

Things are really peaceful now,
in that brownstone house;
You can hear a pin drop,
it's as quiet as a mouse.

Now Charlie goes a-busking
by the River Seine,
or down the Paris metro
if he thinks it looks like rain.

Sometimes he'll head to the Eiffel Tower,
the tourists love him there.
They adore his Parisian accent,
and his glorious head of hair.
With his silk cravat and Vandyke beard
he's oh so debonaire.

He's also got a brand new act
in a Paris cabaret,
but he won't give up the busking,
not yet anyway.

The Eiffel Tower's his favourite spot,
he makes more money there.
He's the darling of the ladies,
so suave and debonaire.

The tourists love to hear the songs
that made Sinatra great,
so when it's time to pay their dues
they never hesitate.

Now Charlie's found a proper job
his little wife, Marie,
doesn't grumble anymore,
she's happy as can be.

She even goes to catch his act
at the Paris cabaret;
She's a great fan of Sinatra now,
and she really digs 'My Way.'

Life is good for Charlie
and his beautiful Marie;
They never want for anything,
they're oh so fancy-free
in that brownstone house in Paris
near the Rue de Rivoli.

May they always have good fortune
as they make their way through life;
Dashing Champagne Charlie,
and his comely little wife.

Champagne Charlie – The Sequel

We're back with Champagne Charlie
and his wife Marie,
In their precious brownstone house
near the Rue De Rivoli.

He still enjoys the busking,
but prefers the cabaret;
Where he flirts with
the topless dancing girls,
to pass the time away.
But it's all so very innocent,
he can't afford to stray.

But Charlie's disenchanted
with the Paris cabaret;
He works his butt off every night
and doesn't get much pay.

One night a big promoter
came to the cabaret;
She offered him a contract,
and Charlie said, 'Okay.'
She winked at him
then shook his hand.
'You're going to be a star,
the biggest thing since Aznavour,
with me you will go far.'

She said, 'You are so handsome,
suave and debonaire;
I love your charming accent,
and your gorgeous head of hair.'

'Come back to my boudoir,'
she whispered tenderly.
Charlie's sorely tempted,
but he's loyal to Marie,
waiting in their love nest
near the Rue De Rivoli.

Now Champagne Charlie's
life has changed, quite dramatically.
But will he be better off?
We'll have to wait and see.

Marie is not too happy,
she loves her simple life;
All she's ever wanted
is to be somebody's wife.

Champagne Charlie's moonstruck
with his new-found fame;
The public all adore him,
the whole world knows his name.

He's left the humble brownstone house,
near the Rue De Rivoli;
Said adieu to the neighbourhood,
deserted sweet Marie.

He's living it up on the Cote D'Azure,
on a million-dollar yacht;
With pretty girls and hangers-on,
he's happy with his lot.

They dine on expensive lobster,
truffles and caviar;
Charlie can afford the best,
now that he's a star.

He visits Vegas twice a year,
with his tribute show;
But the cheering crowds
have dwindled away,
and Charlie has to go.

He's squandered all his fortune,
gambled it away;
He owes the casino big time,
and now he has to pay;
It's sent the debt collectors in,
will Champagne Charlie ever win?

They've seized the million-dollar yacht,
and yellow Maserati;
The hangers-on and pretty girls
no longer want to party.

Charlie's back in Paris now,
living quietly;
Far away from the brownstone house,
and his former wife Marie.

He's playing the piano,
in a nondescript café;
He works there till the early hours,
and stays in bed all day.

Charlie's former sweetheart
has moved on with her life;
She's met an Aussie larrikin,
and soon she'll be his wife.

She's sold the little brownstone house
on the Rue De Rivoli,
and moved to a far-flung
sunburnt land,
across the jewelled sea.

Now it's Au 'voir Champagne Charlie,
may the Gods smile down on you;
As you traverse the rocky highway
of life,
may your wildest dreams come true;
May you always have good fortune,
in everything you do;
So Bon Chance Champagne Charlie,
Adieu Mon Ami Adieu.

Our House

If you should come to our house,
chances are you'll see,
Mickey Mouse and his girl Minnie
waiting patiently.
They've heard that you might visit
and they're happy as can be.

This is an extra special day,
when the toys come out to play;
So step right in, please don't be shy,
we're very glad that you dropped by.

Donald Duck and Daisy too,
with all the other Disney crew
will be on hand to welcome you.
We promise you'll have lots of fun,
there's something here for everyone.

But Goofy's nowhere to be found,
he's underneath the stairs,
Playing hide and seek with Pluto
and the panda bears.

Teddy bears on rocking horses
love to ride all day;
Tin toys make lots of noise.
Music boxes play.

Dolls watch from every corner,
thrilled that they can be
an oh so very special part
of this great big family.

Trains race around the tracks,
cars and trucks abound;
While the dolls all sit,
so entranced by it
that they never make a sound.

But they're really quite excited,
for the circus is in town;
With animals and acrobats,
and a naughty little clown.

The three little pigs are here today,
from the big bad wolf
they've run away.
He blew down their houses,
except for one
so they joined the circus
to have some fun.

Mickey Mouse has turned up too.
He'll show them all what he can do;
Tell a joke or sing a song,
with him in charge
things can't go wrong.

Goofy's still in hiding,
underneath the stairs,
while Pluto searches everywhere,
with the panda bears.

But Goofy has a new best friend,
a pretty Butterfly,
and they tell each other stories,
to help the time pass by.

We hope that you've enjoyed your day
with Mickey and his crew,
all the dolls and other toys
that live in our house too.

Now your visit's over,
and you have gone away.
The Sandman calls upon the toys.
He whispers, 'No more play.
It's time you all were fast asleep,
you've had a busy day.'

Then he sprinkles them with stardust
and quietly slips away.

While the Man in the Moon
smiles down on the world,
and the stars come out to play;
The toys dream of tomorrow
and a bright new sunny day.

Our House – 2

Now you've been to our house,
did you like it there?
The toys enjoyed your visit,
especially George the Bear.

A big old cuddly fellow,
George just wants to play;
He loved the hugs you gave him,
when you called in that day.

Daisy Duck and Donald too,
were pleased as punch to welcome you
on such a bright sunshiny day,
when the toys were all at play.

The dolls were so excited
to see your smiling face;
The tin toys made their usual noise,
it was a rowdy place.

George's teddy family
showed off quite a bit;
The way they rode those horses
really was a hit.

Since you came to visit us,
Pluto and the bears
have found old Goofy
munching apples
underneath the stairs.

Did you enjoy the circus?
We heard that you where there,
Dumbo saw you watching him
as he flew through the air.

What a brave young pachyderm,
it gave us all a scare
to see that little elephant
soaring way up there.

But Dumbo's not afraid at all,
though it's very high;
Perhaps one day he'll leave our house
and fly up to the sky,
where fluffy clouds and giant balloons
silently float by.

Mickey also spied you
from the corner of his eye,
as he loudly beat the bright red drum
while proudly marching by.

We hope that you'll come back again,
you really made our day.
You're welcome here at any time
for as long as you want to stay.

The Busker

The busker sits at her keyboard,
on a radiant summer's day;
She smiles at the people gathering 'round,
then she starts to play.

Nostalgic songs from yesteryear,
when the world was a better place;
When life was so much simpler,
and we moved at a slower pace.

Workers breeze by,
they pause for a while,
throw a few coins
and leave with a smile.

'Can't stop,' they explain,
then scurry away;
Back to the grindstone,
no time for play.

The busker salutes
and winks her eye,
thanks every generous passer-by.

So many songs the busker knows,
hits from the movies and musical shows;
Abba, The Beatles, tunes from the war,
dance numbers, country, love songs
and more.

She plays a catchy number,
and people tap their feet;
Grooving to the rhythm
of the red-hot Latin beat,
one two Cha Cha Cha,
there's dancing in the street.

Some folk form a Conga line,
others clap along;
A cheeky magpie charms the crowd
with his lilting song.

Dear old Murphy's here today,
he's asked the busker if she'll play
some much-loved melodies.
His Irish eyes smile
and his heart fills with joy,
when the busker obliges with 'Danny Boy.'
Then she really makes his day
with 'Molly Malone' and 'Galway Bay.'

George the Greek might be here soon,
'Never on Sunday' is his favourite tune;
He's been a Greek dancer
for most of his life,
along with Maria, his beautiful wife.

Then it's time for the final song,
she asks the crowd to sing along;
She's surely left the best till last,
a bittersweet memory from the past.

We'll meet again,
don't know where, don't know when,
but I know we'll meet again
some sunny day.

Hearts are filled with emotion,
when the busker plays that song;
Old timers wipe the tears from their eyes
and try to sing along.

The music fades but the memory lingers,
it's been a wonderful day;
Three cheers for the busker,
Hip Hip Hooray!

A Place in The Sun

Once in another lifetime,
far from the human race,
you and I found our place in the sun,
untouched by time and space.

Where dark vales hide their secrets,
and high peaks touch the sky;
Where Eos – 'Goddess of the dawn,'
bids the night goodbye.

We've stood below those mighty peaks
and watched the errant skylark
sweep through the dusky shadows
on its way to Shangri-la,
past the Mountains of the Moon,
beyond the Evening Star.

Our nights were filled with passion,
breathless ecstasy,
magic indelible moments in time
when I'd hold you close to me,
and we'd trip the light fantastic
by the unrelenting sea.

We'd gaze in awestruck wonder
at the opalescent rainbow,
alone but never lonely
on that barren sandy shore,
and as I looked into your eyes
I loved you even more.

But soon your wayward restless soul
longed for other places;
To roam unfettered, wild and free,
beneath the sapphire sky;
Through my tears I wished you well,
God speed my love, Goodbye.

In my dreams I've seen your shadow
in a bar in old Havana;
A garish smoky dance hall
down Argentina way;
Where the throbbing music never ends
until the break of day.

How I envied the dark stranger
who took you in his arms,
and danced with you throughout
the night,
spellbound by your charms.

Did I glimpse you strolling blithely
down a boulevard in Paris?
Dining at the Moulin Rouge,
relaxing by the Seine;
Perhaps by chance you watched me
from a gondola in Venice,
as I sheltered from the early
morning rain.

When the time is right we'll meet again,
on our final odyssey;
We'll bid farewell to a crumbling world
of pain and misery;
The awful price mankind has paid
for its inhumanity.

We'll soar where golden eagles dare,
forever wild and free;
To a mystical cloud-topped mountain
above the ageless sea.

We'll climb a radiant stairway,
to search for Shangri-la,
past the Mountains of the Moon,
beyond the Evening Star.

Where a million flickering candles,
like fireflies in the sky,
light up the dark-veiled firmament,
as cherubim float by.

So little skylark guide us there,
to that sacred place;
A lifetime from the world we once knew,
and the selfish human race.

But alas for me it's just a dream,
a haunting reverie
that drifts across my heart-strings
and never sets me free;
Enticing and bewitching,
like an untamed melody.

When the sands of time have faded,
and I've said my last hoorah,
I'll hitch a ride on a moonbeam,
and sail to Shangri-la,
above the shrouded veil of night,
beyond the Evening Star.

Where my spirit will dwell with the
angels in the promised land,
and there my beautiful long-lost love
will be waiting to take my hand.

We'll join the angelic chorus,
at last forever free
to live our lives in Paradise,
for all eternity
as we dance the last waltz together,
my enchanting angel and me.

Mrs Brown

This is the sad and sorry tale
of little Mrs Brown;
A fine upstanding lady
from a pleasant country town.

She moved there just a year ago,
with hubby Mr Brown in tow.
He had just retired, you know
now starts my dismal tale of woe.

They'd bought a brand new caravan
to traverse our great southern land.
A cruise upon the ocean,
was another thing they'd planned.

But fate had dealt a dreadful blow,
the poor old girl's a sad widow;
She stays home instead.
The awesome cruise is cancelled,
and the van stays in the shed.

She spends her days in solitude,
with reruns on TV;
She's oh so very lonely,
full of misery.
She dreams of trips and giant ships
and cries 'most constantly.

Time drags on so slowly,
she feels she's going mad;
She has no friends or family,
it really is quite sad.

But soon it will be different,
road trips and jaunts galore;
She's feeling so much better,
than she did before.

It's been the final showdown
at the bowling club today;
A bowl's widow she is no more,
soon she'll have her way;
Mrs Brown's elated,
time for a holiday.

But hubby's not complaining,
and doesn't seem upset;
He tells his curious little wife,
'I've got good news, my pet.'

Mr Brown explains
with a smile on his face,
'It's bowling next
at the Senior's Place,
Four arvos a week, two nights as well.'
She wishes the bowls would rot
in hell.

'Let's have a drink to celebrate,'
she says, all meek and mild;
But inside she is seething,
feeling very wild.

She slips a mickey into his glass,
watches him sleep, let's the hours pass;
Then places a pillowcase over his head,
and smothers him until he's stone cold dead.

Mrs Brown's a widow again,
a merry one for sure;
She never wants for money now,
she's certainly not poor.

She lives a life of luxury,
on cruise ships every day;
Mrs Brown from a country town,
now does things her own way.

Ship Ahoy Mrs Brown

Remember naughty Mrs Brown,
the merry little widow from a country town?
She used to be a bored housewife,
but now she leads a different life.

Every year her time is spent,
on a different continent.
Mixing with the snobby rich,
while cruising on the sea;
Or sailing on a riverboat,
her life is fancy-free.

But her money has run out,
and for sure, without a doubt,
her carefree days at sea
will soon be o'er;
She'll have to start a brand new life
away from all the glamour;
A bored and lonely land-lubber
once more.

She thinks she'll have to hatch a plan
to find herself a rich old man;
Make him think she's wealthy too,
that shouldn't be so hard to do.

Then fate stepped in that very night,
she chanced upon a Mr White;
A millionaire so she was told,
a dear old man with a heart of gold.

But Mr White was hunting too,
for a lonely gal who was well-to-do;
When he saw Mrs Brown looking so fine,
dripping with furs and jewellery divine,
he plied her with expensive wine,
said to himself, 'This woman is mine.'

He was told Mrs Brown had money to burn,
but alas, Mr White had a lot to learn;
He wined and dined her every night,
he thought he'd found his Mrs Right.

Mrs Brown wasn't the marrying kind,
she had just one thing on her mind;
To take his money and leave
him behind;
Dead or alive she didn't much care,
he meant nothing to her,
this old millionaire.

Then one night Mr White
who was not very bright,
suggested they change their wills;
She agreed right away,
'Let's do it today, before our ship
reaches land.'

The deed was soon done,
Mrs Brown thought she'd won;
Her next move was not very nice,
'Dearest,' she told him,
'I've champagne on ice,'
'Let's drink to our future,
our blissful new life;
When we get together
as husband and wife.'

Mr White moaned, after a spell,
'I need some fresh air,
I feel so unwell.'
Naughty little Mrs Brown
suggested with a smile,
'Let's go up to the pool deck,
we could make out for a while.'

Her idea was so enticing,
he could hardly wait,
and sadly in the hot tub,
the poor man met his fate;
Just like naive Mr Brown
in the prime of his life
she cut him down.

They found him in the morning,
just as the day was dawning,
'Accidental drowning,'
was what the doctor said.
'We'll have to tell his lady friend
her fiancée is dead.'

Mrs Brown was overcome,
so many tears she shed;
'Please don't tell me that it's so,
my dearest one is dead.
We were so very happy,
planning to be wed.'

She could have won an Oscar,
her acting was so good;
Our wicked little lady,
should go to Hollywood.

Of course she's laughing inside,
if only people knew;
She has plans to buy a yacht
and sail the ocean blue;
With a hunky toy-boy,
or maybe even two.

But the tide's gone out for Mrs Brown,
her cruising days are o'er;
She'll have to chart
a different course,
somewhere back on shore.

For it turns out that Mr White,
wasn't well to do;
He was charming, smooth
and debonaire,
a con-man, not a millionaire.

Such a fortunate lass is Mrs Brown,
she won't let anything
get her down;
She's gone back to cruising,
but these days she gets paid;
She's found herself a cushy job,
as a rich old lady's maid.

Her generous employer
is rapt in Mrs Brown;
'You're such a willing worker,
you've never let me down.'

'I have no friends or family,
I'm a widow too.
So yesterday I changed my will,
and left the lot to you.'

How very nice for Mrs Brown,
but goodness gracious me,
let's hope the dear old lady
won't be victim number three,
as her naughty maid prepares
her special blend of Earl Grey Tea.

But Mrs Brown has mellowed,
she's quite prepared to wait
until her benefactor
has reached her use-by date.

Then one night her mistress
died quite peacefully;
Mrs Brown felt very sad,
the poor old girl was not so bad.

The whole wide world's her oyster,
now she's a millionaire;
She could join the jet set,
and travel everywhere.

She thinks that she might settle down,
somewhere back on land;
Buy a splendid French chateau,
or a manor grand.

The French chateau was not the go,
for little Mrs Brown;
She's opted for a mansion,
near a small provincial town.

She's a picture of contentment,
at last she's settled down;
So it's goodbye, farewell for now,
to Little Mrs Brown.

Mamma Mia Mrs Brown

I bet you thought you heard the last
of little Mrs Brown;
Who bought herself a stately home
near a quiet provincial town;
A virtuous old lady now,
she's finally settled down.

But she still delights in trips abroad,
to Rome and gay Paree;
While Monte Carlo in the spring
is where she likes to be;
Living the life of Riley,
in the lap of luxury,
and oh the joys of tasting wine
in the hills of Tuscany.

She never tires of the northern
lights
in the Land of the Midnight Sun,
and the Taj Mahal at evenfall,
when the day is almost done.
But time and tide are ebbing away
for little Mrs Brown;
She's had to stop her travelling,
and try to settle down.

One fateful day in Venice,
a handsome gondolier
smiled at Mrs Brown and won
her heart;
He was a Casanova, a selfish Romeo,
with an eye for rich old ladies;
A shameless gigolo.

He serenaded Mrs Brown
and gave her everything,
from dodgy Chinese perfume
to a worthless emerald ring.

Mrs Brown was starry-eyed,
floating on cloud nine;
When Romeo saw that she was hooked,
he fed her his usual line.

After a candlelight dinner
and too much cheap red wine,
he held her hand and whispered,
'How I wish you could be mine.'

'You are my one and only love,
and I want to marry you.
But I have a wife already,
and several children too.'

'I guess this means we'll have to end
our precious love affair,
for I am just a simple man,
I'm not a millionaire.'

Mrs Brown was mesmerised,
she really did not care
that he had no riches
nor worldly goods to share;
To lose her handsome Romeo
was more than she could bear.

'Come home with me my darling,
and we'll live in luxury;
You'll never want for anything
as long as you're with me.'
So they settled down and Mrs Brown
was the talk of all the town.

She made a cosy love-nest
with her charming Romeo
and tongues would wag and fingers point
wherever she would go;
But she didn't give a damn
because she loved him so.

But good things never seem to last,
and Romeo was tiring fast;
'You silly gullible old dame,
dull by nature and by name;
I'll take you to the cleaners
for half of all you've got,
and maybe if I'm lucky
I might even get the lot.'

But naughty little Mrs Brown
knew just what to do;
'I'll give you anything you want,
I'm also tired of you.
Why don't we have a glass of wine,
and talk this matter through.'

Romeo thought that he had won,
but alas he'd brought himself undone;
It never pays to cross our Mrs Brown.
The red wine tasted rather strange,
her victim didn't care,
thinking that he'd soon be rich,
a multi-millionaire.

He should have stayed in Italy,
where he would still be fancy-free;
But greed and lust for wealth
had let him down,
and the only one who's laughing
is wicked Mrs Brown.

The good folk in the little town
were very sad for Mrs Brown;
Her handsome young Italian
had packed his bags and left,
leaving her despondent,
forlorn and quite bereft;
But the old girl wasn't sad for long,
soon she was singing a different
song.

She has a brand new hobby now,
does little Mrs Brown;
Her veggie patch is something
to behold;
Her spinach, beans and broccoli
are quite a sight to see,
her cabbages are worth
their weight in gold.

She wins all the prizes
at every rural show,
and when the judges ask her
how she manages to grow
the most colossal pumpkins
in the land,
'I'm not supposed to tell you,
I'm sure you understand.'

'It's a secret recipe
that my lover gave to me
before he went and left me all alone.'
But there was no secret recipe,
just one ingredient:
the very best Italian Blood and Bone.

So gentlemen please heed my plea:
if you meet Mrs Brown,
don't take a drink alone with her,
she might just bring you down.

She seems a sweet old lady,
but don't be taken in;
She's a cunning little shyster,
who always has to win.

Bon Voyage Mrs Brown

Mrs Brown was feeling down,
unhappy with her lot,
so she went on a spending spree
and bought a swanky yacht.

A smart new wardrobe was the go,
the kind that Admirals wear;
She thought that if she looked the part
she'd bag a millionaire.

Yes Mrs Brown's still on the prowl,
to capture Mr Right;
For sure it wasn't Romeo,
or poor old Mr White.

She hired a motley all-girl crew
to help her sail the yacht;
But little did she know that they
had hatched a deadly plot;
They planned to stage a mutiny
and dump her body in the sea.

But walls have ears, and Mrs Brown
had overheard the plot;
'How dare they double-cross me,
I'll fix this little lot.'
Yes when you cross our Mrs Brown,
be careful or she'll bring you down.

She went down to the galley
and mixed a fearsome brew
into a tasty casserole, a hearty chicken stew.
'Come along you lucky girls, have I a treat for you.'

She plied them with the scrumptious food,
and lots of beer and wine;
The girls had no suspicions,
they thought that things were fine.

They closed their eyes and sailed away
into eternal rest;
Mrs Brown had won again,
she's better than the best.

Mrs Brown hung around
to make sure they were dead;
By now she was feeling quite tipsy,
and tottered off to bed.

She grabbed a magnum of champagne
to keep her company;
She'll be sorry in the morning,
just you wait and see.

She awoke next morning
and stumbled from her bed;
I have to have some food, she thought,
to clear my aching head.

She staggered to the galley,
and spied the chicken stew;
'My word, that looks delicious,
I'll have a plate or two.'

Mrs Brown was ravenous,
she had lost the plot;
In her drunken stupor,
she had clean forgot
the deadly mixture she had added
to the cooking pot.

She sat among the corpses
and finished off the stew;
She thought it had a strange exotic taste
but it was so delectable
she didn't care one bit;
She couldn't bear to see it go to waste.

Then too late she realised
the stupid thing she'd done;
'Oh dearie me,' cried Mrs Brown,
'This time I haven't won.'
Her liking for the demon drink
had brought her right undone.

The old dame and her girly crew
have popped their clogs,
said toodle-oo;
Revenge is sweet so people say,
and Romeo got his today,
as did Mr White and Mr Brown.

At last we'll say farewell, adieu,
to little Mrs Brown;
Whose wicked ways and lust for life
have finally brought her down.

I wonder if she's with Saint Peter
at the Pearly Gates,
or stoking red-hot embers down in Hell;
It doesn't really matter,
but if it is the latter,
Mrs Brown should manage very well.

Epitaph

Here lies the body of Daffodil Brown
In the prime of life
she was cruelly cut down
She made a mistake, a terrible blunder
Now she's pushing up daisies
Six Feet Under.

Dapper Dan

This is the tale of Dapper Dan,
handsome and charming, a smooth ladies' man;
The big shots at his bowls club
have banned poor Dan for life;
He got caught playing extra ends
with the President's buxom wife.

They handed Dan a farewell gift
which caught him by surprise;
Crash, Wallop - what a mess,
two beautiful black eyes.

He'll have to lay low for a little while,
it wouldn't be very wise
to let the ladies see him
with his glorious ebony eyes.

I hope Dan's learnt his lesson,
don't fool with another man's wife;
If you get caught with your pants down,
it'll only bring you strife.

Perhaps he's learnt his lesson,
he's courting a lass called Shirl;
She's not a thing of beauty,
but she is a single girl.

He still has an eye for the ladies,
but can't afford to stray,
for Shirl is a red-hot wrestler,
and practices every day;
At six-foot two and twice his size,
Shirl has the final say.

He's joined another bowls club
and Shirley tags along;
She has to make sure he stays in line
and doesn't do her wrong.

They're getting hitched tomorrow,
Shirl's in the family way;
Let's hope the baby looks like Dan,
or there'll be hell to pay.

For Shirl's been cheating on poor Dan,
with not just one bloke but two;
A pair of Asian immigrants,
Dim Sim and Vindaloo.

Five months later came the birth,
not just one babe but three;
Yellow, brown and milky white,
said Dan, 'How can this be,
that two of them are Asian,
and just one looks like me?'

Shirl told a fishy story
about her family tree,
'I have Chinese and Indian blood
in my ancestry.'

Great grandmother was Indian,
Calcutta born and bred;
She fell in love with a Chinese boy,
and one day they were wed.

Her far-fetched yarn was laughable,
but Dan was not amused.
He thought her tale was rubbish,
and asked to be excused.

He trudged on home and packed his bags,
a far more wiser man.
Farewelled his friends and hit the road
in his trusty kombi van.

Time has passed and our friend Dan
is at peace with the world,
a contented man;
He'll soon be taking custody
of a bonny little girl,
with russet hair and milky skin,
unlike her mother Shirl;
The apple of her daddy's eye,
a rare and precious pearl.

At long last Dan has settled down,
as happy as can be
in a Spanish hacienda by the deep blue sea,
with a dark-eyed senorita
who will soon be his wife;
She'll be a mother to his bairn
and keep Dan out of strife.

So 'Vaya Con Dios' and Adios
to Dan and his family;
They're living life to the fullest
by the unrelenting sea,
in their Spanish hacienda,
what a glorious place to be.

The Greedy Widow

There was a young farmer called Ned,
whose wife dyed his hair blazing red,
his prize bull went mad
when it saw Ned's red hair,
now his poor wife's a widow,
how very unfair.

What a demise farmer Ned,
I'm sorry to say that he's still very dead;
His widow's gone fishing,
she's reeling in,
a bald millionaire, as ugly as sin.

They met in the springtime,
next summer they wed;
She bought him a toupee
to hide his bald head,
a horrible thing in a shade of bright red.

She flattered his ego,
'So handsome,' she said;
He was happy as Larry
and chased her to bed,
that gullible bridegroom was easily led.

But – 'Not tonight Darling,
I've got a bad head.
Why don't you go for a nice walk instead?'

He did as she said,
and the next day turned up dead;
The flea-ridden hair-piece
still on his bald head;
Sadly he met the same fate as poor Ned.
Can someone please tell me
why bulls don't like red?

The baneful black widow was not at all sad,
as a matter of fact she was awfully glad;
Did she commit the perfect crime?
Did the bull get the blame for the second time?
The cops were bamboozled,
so called in Scotland Yard,
who soon cracked the case,
it wasn't too hard.

So crime didn't pay
for this loathsome young wife;
Justice prevailed
and she's banged-up for life.

The bull is in clover,
free from all blame,
with a harem of ladies,
he's become rather tame.

My tale has a moral:
if your hair is red,
don't tangle with mad bulls,
you might end up dead;
And gents, don't trust widows
with greed in their eyes,
you may just be in
for a nasty surprise.

Franklin Fife's Folly

This is the tale of Franklin Fife,
also known as Frank;
A highly paid executive
in an international bank.

He lives in a New York penthouse
with his greedy nagging wife.
He's a millionaire twice over
and they lead a lavish life.
But hang on, hold your horses,
it looks like Frank's in strife.

Madam's bored to death with Frank,
she thinks that he's a joke.
She's set her sights on another man,
a well-endowed young bloke.

It's time to call a spade a spade
and ask for a divorce;
Then she'll be on easy street,
filthy-rich of course.

She'll take him to the cleaners,
and she doesn't care
that Frank will have no money,
which isn't very fair.

But Franklin isn't stupid,
he's engaged the best.
The finest lawyers in the land
to rid him of this pest,
who used to be a loving wife
but now just wants to cause him strife.

The expensive lawyers won the case,
the wife got nothing at all;
No car, no jewels, not even the dog,
Franklin's having a ball;
On easy street for the rest of his life,
no cares, no worries, no nagging wife.

He celebrates with French champagne
and oysters every night,
but after an evening of gluttony,
Frank didn't feel quite right;
Early next morning the poor man was dead,
A batch of bad oysters, the post-mortem said.

Now Franklin's met his maker,
in Paradise up high;
Hanging around on a fluffy white cloud,
watching angels floating by;
Hitching a ride on a vagrant star,
in an azure tinted sky.

Sprinkling the world with stardust
to make it a better place;
But sadly there's not enough stardust
to save the human race.

As for his greedy former wife,
she's certainly okay;
Driving a red Ferrari,
new outfits every day;
Living with her toy boy
in the lap of luxury,
'cause Frank forgot to change his will,
how stupid can you be?

The Soldier's Wife

She threw a kiss to her soldier boy
as he marched off to the war,
to join his fellow countrymen
who had boldly gone before,
to face a fearsome enemy
on a barren bloody shore.

He was only twenty-three,
but he wanted to keep his homeland free
from a terrible despot's tyranny,
so he left his wife and newfound life
to do his bit for the war,
just as his father, his childhood hero,
had done some years before.

His letters were filled with sadness and woe,
of mates that were lost to a dark dreaded foe;
But he wrote not to worry, that he'd be okay,
he hoped to come home soon,
he longed for that day.

He'd write of his love for his beautiful wife,
for she was the reason he still clung to life.
He cherished her letters,
they made his heart smile;
Just the thought of her love
made living worthwhile.
He prayed for the moment
he'd hold her again,
when life would no longer
be filled with such pain.

She dreamed of him often,
come rain or shine;
Her handsome young soldier,
he seemed to be fine.
She'd reach out to him,
but alas he had gone
back to the fighting that raged on and on.

Then in her dreams, one dark moonless night,
there appeared at her bedside
a vision in white;
A heavenly seraphim, an angel of light,
'I bring you a message from one very dear.
He'll always be with you, forever near.
Be happy for him, at last he's at rest,
for God only takes the brightest and the best.'

'Look into the night sky, you'll see a bright star,
it will follow you always, wherever you are;
And I will be there to watch over you,
to keep you from harm, to help you pull through.'

Then the angel arose in a halo of light,
so lustrous and golden, in the dark sacred
night;
Through the deep velvet curtain,
of the indigo sky,
where star spangled moonbeams
drift silently by.

The soldier's wife woke to a grey wintery morn,
recalling her dream she felt downcast, forlorn;
Was it an omen, a sign from above,
to tell her she'd lost her only true love?

The steadfast young wife got on with her life,
though she feared that knock
on her door
that so many loving families
had heard at least once before.
The sound that preceded the fateful news
of another young soul lost to war.

One dreary day a telegram came,
'missing in action' it read;
But she already knew deep down in her heart
that her soldier boy was dead;
Another young life lost in vain to the war,
silently sleeping, in pain no more;
Forever at peace on a distant shore.

She's older now and all alone,
she's never found love again;
She could not bear to lose another,
it would have caused her too much pain;
She sits in her shabby old rocking chair
and dreams of her soldier boy,
her brown-eyed loveable larrikin
who brought her so much joy.

She dreads that one day of the year,
when comrades march and children cheer.
The bands play the tunes all over again,
'Pack Up Your Troubles,' and 'Lilli Marlene'
while hardened men shed a vagrant tear
and promise their mates they'll be back
next year.

She'd rather recall in solitude
the ones who had gone before;
Heroes asleep in that vale of tears
on a dim and distant shore,
because of man's inhumanity
and a cruel barbaric war.
Then she closes her tired eyes again,
soon she'll be free from grief and pain.

The autumn leaves are dying,
winter has set in;
There's no-one left to mourn her,
she hasn't kith or kin;
She sleeps beneath a stark white cross,
under southern skies,
far away from the verdant fields
where her sweetheart lies.

But her spirit soars through the velvet sky,
beyond the midnight sun
to abide with her beloved,
to always be as one;
Riding the crest of a rainbow,
forever wild and free,
until the very end of time,
for all eternity.

When the weary world is sleeping,
in the quiet of the night,
two stars ignite the heavens
with a lustrous blinding light;
Two celestial beings
in the darkness high above,
tragic star-crossed lovers,
re-united by their love.

Two radiant spirits together at last
free from the heartache
and pain of the past;
Two waxing stars in the cosmos above,
parted by fate, united by love;
Aglow in the darkness,
at last side by side,
a brave unsung hero
and his loving bride.

Why?

In a peaceful corner of the world,
poppies bloom again;
Caressed by the golden sunlight,
kissed by the gentle rain;
Where valiant heroes, young and old,
gave their lives in vain.

They fought there on those blood-soaked fields,
so many years ago;
'The war to end all wars,' 'twas said,
but how could people know
that this was not the final time
the world would be at war?
That men would still die on the killing fields,
as they had done before.

So many lives have been sacrificed
in the name of liberty;
What would they think, those selfless souls,
if only they could see
that the world they left so long ago
is still no longer free?

A mother weeps and a father mourns
for the loss of their only son;
A faithful wife prays through the lonely night,
'Please spare my beloved one.'
Children stand at the window
and wait for their father's return;
A grief-stricken widow cries out in the gloom,
'Why won't mankind ever learn?'

On a cold and dismal autumn morn,
the bugle sounds in the early dawn;
We come to honour those dauntless souls
who never came back to our shore;
We salute the countless women and men
who still go off to war
so we can live in harmony,
forever at peace, once again free.

Far away in Flander's Fields
where brave men fought in vain,
Poppies bloom in the noonday sun,
life goes on again;
Lovers stroll down quiet lanes,
dreaming, hand in hand;
The sound of children's laughter
echoes o'er the timeless land.

But mothers still grieve and widows weep,
a young child moans in his restless sleep;
A father wipes the tears from his eyes
as he prays for his son's return;
While a lone voice cries out
in the wilderness,
'When will mankind ever learn?'

Maybe

The old lady, deep in silent thought,
gazes out at the timeless sea,
how she envies the gulls as they glide on the wind,
wild and eternally free.
The purple-tinged mountains seem to rise up forever
into a faraway land,
and small children squeal with joyous delight,
building castles in the sand.

She's gazed at this vista over the years,
through good times and bad,
laughter and tears;
Once there were three of them,
a lifetime ago,
she and her Charlie
and the child they loved so.

But children grow restless,
they need to move on
and one day the light of their life had gone
far away from the mountains,
the ageless blue sea,
to fly like a white dove,
wild and free.

But she said she'd come back,
maybe one day in spring,
when the wild roses bloom
and the red robins sing.
But spring becomes summer,
autumn leaves turned to gold,
She never returned
back home to the fold.

She sent letters and cards from far away,
and a virginal flower every May;
A single white rose on the same day each year,
for the mother she loved,
so precious and dear.

Her letters were filled with such utter joy,
she'd fallen in love with a beautiful boy;
So handsome and caring, he made her heart sing,
perhaps we will come back, one day in the spring.

But nothing lasts forever,
roses fade and die;
The letters and cards never came anymore,
her loved ones wondered why.
Perhaps she's found her place in the sun,
where errant sea birds fly,
a far off exotic island
where life passes slowly by.

But even an island paradise
hold secrets dark and grim,
now she rots in a dark and dingy room,
no golden sunlight, only gloom.
There's an old world-weary padre,
who stays with her awhile,
With tears in her eyes
and a heavy heart,
she tries so hard to smile.

She presses a letter into his hand,
'Can you send this message for me?
To that special place where my heart lies,
under azure-tinted skies,
where purple-tinged mountains sweep down to the sea
and wild gulls fly, forever free.'

My dearest ones, don't cry for me,
I've found my place in the sun,
and I'll meet my maker with dignity
when my race has finally been run;
In this dark place I've shed so many tears,
I've missed you over the long, lonely years.

You gave me life a long time ago
and I caused you so much pain,
but I promise I'll come back in the spring,
and we'll all be together again.

The winds of change blow softly,
o'er the mountains and the sea;
Wild geese, untainted and pure,
fly home, unfettered and free.
The old lady closes her tired eyes,
and in her reverie,
remembers the girl who left so long ago,
who needed to be free,
who shattered her loving parents' hearts,
brought them sorrow and misery.

Her nightmares come back to haunt her again,
her life is filled with unending pain.
Sadly the child who's been gone for so long
will never again hear the robin's sweet song.

But she did come back to them in the spring,
when the wild roses bloom and the red robins sing.
Now she looks at the world with unseeing eyes,
in hallowed ground she peacefully lies,
where white roses bloom in the heat of the day,
under clear blue summer skies,
in that place where the mountains sweep down to the sea,
she sleeps forever, finally free.

Reminiscence

I'm growing old and frailer now,
my memory's fading fast;
But I still remember many things,
from the dim and distant past.

I remember a girl with flowing red hair,
ruby red lips and sparkling green eyes;
How she could tempt me, bewitch and beguile me,
oh how she could tantalise
with her flame-coloured hair, milky white skin
and dazzling emerald eyes.

She was a gypsy, hot blooded and free;
I was a dreamer but she loved only me;
She gave up her roaming and we settled down
in a tiny white cottage near a small seaside town.

Our lives were enriched by a wee baby boy,
a redhead so perfect, our pride and our joy,
with creamy white skin and bright eyes so green,
the most beautiful baby that we'd ever seen.

That baby grew into a sweet loving child,
like his mother, a gypsy, unfettered and wild;
He would ride like the wind on a stallion pure white,
roam through the forest from dawn's early light;
But the night was my time with my own special boy,
memorable moments that filled me with joy.

He would listen in awe to the tales that I told,
of villains and heroes, ships loaded with gold,
songs from my childhood, stories of old,
magical unicorns with gossamer wings,
swashbuckling pirates, dragons and kings.

Then he'd drift off to sleep with an angelic smile,
and I'd stay by his bedside for just a short while,
watching my cherub, my pride and my joy,
my reason to smile, my bonny wee boy.
Then slowly our carefree beautiful child
seemed to be different, he no longer smiled.
He never returned to the forest again;
Our sweet baby boy was in terrible pain.

I would kneel at his bedside and utter a prayer,
'Please Lord don't take him, it doesn't seem fair,
his pain and suffering are too much to bear.
I've had a good life, please take me instead,'
and I wept in my sorrow as I knelt by his bed.
'He's only a child, he deserves to be free,
again Lord I'm asking, please won't you take me?'

But my prayers went unanswered,
our child slipped away,
into the darkness one terrible day.
'Don't cry for me Papa,'
he whispered to me.
'And Mama be happy, at last I am free,
of the terrible sadness I've had for a while,
just look to the heavens and try hard to smile.'

'For I'll be in a place where I'll never grow old,
never be lonely, never be cold,
Perhaps there'll be forests
where I can run free,
with white doves and unicorns,
so don't cry for me.'

'But Papa who'll tell me the stories I love,
when you're not with me in that place up above?
Who'll sing me lullabies and tuck me into bed?'
I smiled through my tears and tenderly said,
'I'm sure there's a beautiful angel in white,
who'll tell you stories and kiss you goodnight.'

'But she won't tell me stories like you used to do.
Oh Papa I wish that you could come too,
and Mama I'm scared but I'll try not to cry.
Please hold me forever and kiss me goodbye.'
So we held him close though the long
lonely night
and just after sunrise he lost his brave
fight.

Our hearts were shattered, never to mend,
for my red-headed gypsy this was the end
of the life she once knew with her beautiful boy.
No happiness now, no laughter or joy.

Her passion for life had faded away,
with nothing to live for, no reason to stay;
I found her asleep in the forest one day,
she died of a broken heart they say.

Now they slumber together, forever as one,
but their spirits roam free past the eternal sun;
Over the rainbow, the bright evening star;
I pray that they're happy wherever they are,
perhaps where there's stardust
and moonbeams so bright,
that light up the dark sky, the infinite night.

One day I'll join them, my spirit will fly
up to the heavens through the deep purple sky;
Once more I will be with my gypsy so fair
and my beautiful boy with the curly red hair;
We will walk in the sunshine, laugh in the rain,
we'll never be sad or lonely again.

So I'll wait patiently till it's my time to go,
to leave this old world, make the climb from below;
Over the rainbow, the bright evening star,
to be with my angels wherever they are.

The Quirky Tale of Quentin Quail

Quentin Quail's a wholesome bloke,
who lives on the river bank;
But believe it or not,
for a couple of years,
he smelt like a septic tank;
I'm afraid his breath was just as bad,
it was quite bizarre and very sad.

He used to wear Chanel perfume
and indulge in a bubble bath,
but one grey day in late July,
his life took a different path.

He had a wife, the love of his life,
but she didn't like him at all;
She split with a travelling
salesman,
by the name of Petronius Paul.

Quentin was a broken man,
he loved that woman so,
but Queenie Quail was bored
to tears,
'twas time for her to go;
'Let him find another wife,
to join him in his dead-end life.'

I say it's good riddance
to that cheating wife;
Quentin Quail is better off,
without her in his life.

Quentin's world was looking grim,
there was nothing left for him.
He had no inclination
to take a bath again.
Or even brush his pearly whites,
his heart was racked with pain.

When my love comes back to me,
I'll take a bath, just wait and see;
I'll douse myself with French cologne,
put highlights through my hair.
Then I'll dress up to the nines,
I'll be so debonaire.

Meanwhile Queenie's having fun,
since she flew the coop.
She's dumped the travelling
salesman
and joined a rock'n'roll group.

She's learning to play the tambourine
and thinks that's really cool.
She's fallen for the drummer,
a certain Tyson Tool.

It's been two years
since Queenie Quail
and her salesman hit the road,
Quentin's had enough of the stink
in his river bank abode.

Quentin Quail has given in,
he's stopped his silly stance;
He's bathing thirty times a week,
and looking for romance.
His pearly whites are sparkling bright,
he cleans them morning, noon and night.

He's found a lovely lady
to join him in his shack;
Quentin Quail's a happy man,
he's never looking back.

They're getting married in the spring,
I hope they never part.
Quentin and his sweetie-pie,
the lass who won his heart.

As for Quentin's former wife,
she's given her drummer the flick
and wed a travelling preacher man,
the kindly Simon Schick.
Now she's a born-again Christian,
enjoying her newfound life,
roaming the byways and highways
as a travelling preacher's wife.

Our Love

Our love is like a breath of fresh air
on a warm summer's day;
An incandescent light
shining throughout the dark ethereal night.

Our love will see us through good times
and bad, through storms and tempests,
through the seasons of our life together.

The love that we share flows like
a mighty river on its journey of discovery
to the deep blue timeless sea.

When the ebon velvet curtain of night
descends upon the waiting earth,
our love will light up the heavens like
the evening star.

For our love is an eternal flame burning
brightly in our hearts forever,
until the end of time.

Like the unfettered vagrant snowbird
that makes its pilgrimage over the deep
dark oceans of the night, our love
knows no boundaries, no borders.

So in the mists of time,
when other loves have withered and died,
our love will endure
until our two hearts no longer beat as one;
Until the music of life
fades away and is no more.

Until the infinite silver stars in
God's heaven cease to shine,
and the world grows cold.

The Old Man

The old man sees with misty eyes,
young lovers;
Arm in arm, hand in hand,
fanciful, passionate, in a world of their own,
and the old man remembers!

Remembers another lover, another time;
When just her perfume, cheap perfume,
could send his senses reeling.
Feelings deep inside, hunger, ecstasy.
Yes he was young once, and so was she
and the old man remembers!

Hair like spun silk, black as the night,
glistening in the hot summer sun.
Lips sweet as honey, warm and inviting.
Soft brown skin, bewitching brown eyes,
and the old man remembers!

But sometimes love is not enough,
and the old man remembers!

He remembers how suddenly she was gone,
like the winter winds before a warm spring day.
Never to return, and still he wonders why;
Gone was the love that he thought would never die.

Then the old man remembers;
Other lovers, other feelings, misty memories;
Days of pure enchantment etched deep inside his soul.
Then he cries out for the old loves,
the dear loves, the lost loves,
and the old man remembers!

She

She; In her soliloquy, in her every solitary
waking hour sits haunted by memories,
by ghosts from the distant past.

She remembers long forgotten lovers,
long forgotten feelings,
old familiar feelings.

She stares wistfully
at old ragged photographs,
dusty and neglected over so many years.

With clouded unseeing eyes she gazes
into the mirror. Eyes that once sparkled
like diamonds. Sad faded eyes now.
Once the whole world was dazzled by
her radiance, her ethereal beauty.
Young men flocked to her side like bees
to honey, hypnotised, bewitched by
her charms.

She remembers the young men who
valiantly joined their comrades to fight
for their beloved country;
Some never to return,
sleeping for eternity in a bleak
unforgiving foreign land.

Far away from the verdant hills of home.
She remembers other times, other young
men and how she broke each one's heart,
never caring how she hurt them.
So they drifted away to find new loves
and she was left alone with only
memories. Bittersweet memories.

Now, in the autumn of her life, in her
twilight years, in her loneliness
and her heartache – she remembers.

Friendship

Beyond the hustle and bustle of city life,
far from the madding crowd,
is a haven for the not so young,
the not so old and the young at heart.

Here in this special place there is shelter from the searing
summer heat and the cold winter winds.

Behind the modest unassuming façade our senior citizens
have found a place to call their own.

Over the years battles have been won and lost
in games of skill and chance;
Countless friendships have been made.
Many lives have been changed forever.

Who can be sad here when there is
so much joy, so much laughter?

But sometimes, amid the camaraderie and all the happiness there is sorrow and sadness.

Alas, time and tide wait for no-one, and we mourn those dear members who departed from this world to another place.

We salute others on their brave fight against adversity and pain. We admire their courage and pray for them.

We marvel at each member's every milestone
and celebrate with them.

We are evergreen. We are timeless, enduring, unfading.
We are the world. We are forever young.
Forever wise.

We are proud to be Senior Citizens.

Memories

Remember when we held each other tight
until dawn's early light;
Watching the radiant sun ascend
over the distant mountains.
Remember how we cried when we heard
our special song — our stardust melody;
Remember.

I remember your face, the laughter in your eyes,
and your smile; bewitching, enchanting,
the key to Paradise.
You could light up the darkest hour
with that smile;
I remember too the pain in your eyes
when I hurt you with some meaningless
thought.

Remember how we danced the night away,
wrapped in each other's arms,
like Fred and Ginger
in some old forgotten movie;
How we could trip the light fantastic.

Remember that lonely windswept hill,
where we gazed in awe
and childlike wonder at the beauty
of a rainbow in the heavens;
And like Dorothy, wondered if we also
could soar like birds
over that glorious arc.

Remember how we wrote each other
words of love on scraps of paper;
Oh how we would smile at such exquisite,
fanciful thought;
Remember how we cried
when we sensed that things had changed.

Somehow we had grown apart;
Maybe we had become stronger,
maybe weaker; who knows.

No more love letters,

poetry scribbled in haste;

No more talking till dawn

or watching the sunrise;

No rainbows or dreams of tomorrow.

But we have the Memories,

and like the last waltz

they will endure Forever.

Two Different Worlds

Once, a lifetime ago,
two weary travellers on the lonely
highway of life fell in love.
Once, on a warm summer's day,
two souls came together as one
and love grew and blossomed
like a red, red rose.

But now, like the dying embers
of a winter's fire,
like an ebb tide, a broken melody,
love has gone;
Vanished into the mists of time,
never to return.

Maybe they were not to be,
those tragic star-crossed lovers.
Maybe far too different,
too set in their ways.

For her there was no Camelot,
no knight in shining armour;
For him no fairy princess,
no angel of the morning.

While the silver stars salute
the dark sacred night,
while the celestial moon
keeps a silent vigil on the world below,
she remembers the love that they had,
the unforgettable magic moments
that they once shared.

She wipes a vagrant tear
from her cheek, and she wonders
if he too is lonely,
if he has found someone new
on that lonesome highway of life.

Through My Window

Through my window I see
grey lifeless bitumen,
cold, uninviting;
Going nowhere, yet ending somewhere.
No verdant rolling pastures here.

A solitary ebon woman, barefoot,
deep in thought, wanders aimlessly
along the dusty uneven footpath;
A stranger, not unlike me,
in an alien landscape.

www.ingramcontent.com/pod-product-compliance
Lightning Source LLC
Chambersburg PA
CBHW021149080526
44588CB00008B/269